Second Edition

Cambridge Primary Path 1

Grammar and Writing Workbook

Sarah Dilger

Contents

Unit	Grammar	Learn to Write	Writing
1 What is a family? page 3	Verb *to be*, Affirmative and Negative Verb *to be*, Yes/No Questions	Basic Capitalization	You and Your Family
2 What is school like? page 13	Demonstrative Pronouns: *this*, *that*, *these*, *those* Possessive Adjectives	Question Marks	Questions to Ask a New Student
3 What are living things? page 23	*There is*, *there are* Prepositions of Place: *in*, *on*, *under*, *next to*	Commas	Living Things in a Backyard

Unit 1–3 Review page 93

Unit	Grammar	Learn to Write	Writing
4 What is a friend? page 33	Present Simple: Affirmative and Negative Present Simple: Yes/No Questions	Capital Letters and Periods	A Friend
5 How do we have fun? page 43	Present Simple: *like*, *likes*, *don't like*, *doesn't like* Possessive *'s*	Exclamation Points	Fun Activities
6 How can we help? page 53	Present Simple: *have*, *has*, Affirmative and Negative Present Simple: *have*, *has*, Wh- Questions	Nouns	People, Places, and Things

Unit 4–6 Review page 94

Unit	Grammar	Learn to Write	Writing
7 Why do we need plants and animals? page 63	*Can*, *can't* Countable and Uncountable Nouns	Verbs	Descriptions
8 What is imagination? page 73	Present Simple: *want / need*, Affirmative and Negative Present Simple: *want / need*, Wh- Questions	Adjectives	Description of a Picture
9 Why do we need clothes? page 83	Present Progressive: Affirmative and Negative Present Progressive: Yes/No Questions	Adverbs	How People Are Doing Things

Unit 7–9 Review page 95

1 What is a family?

Grammar: Verb *to be*, Affirmative and Negative

ePals

Country **Brazil**

Hello. I'm Sonya, and I'm from Brazil!

I'm seven years old. I have two sisters. Juliana is twelve. Marcia is nine. We live with our parents in an apartment. It isn't big, but it's near the beach. I go to the beach on the weekends with my family. My cousins come, too. They aren't from Brazil. They're from Colombia. My family is big, and we have lots of fun together.

1 Where does Sonya go on the weekends?

2 Underline the affirmative forms of *to be*.
   a   I'm Sonya, and I'm from Brazil.
   b   Juliana is twelve, and Marcia is nine.
   c   It isn't big, but it's near the beach.
   d   They aren't from Brazil. They're from Colombia.

Grammar: Verb *to be*, Affirmative and Negative

We use the verb *to be* to talk about facts:

Juana **is** nine.
She**'s** from Mexico.
She **isn't** Chinese.

Mustapha and Aykut **are** Turkish.
They**'re** friends.
They **aren't** brothers.

I **am** Pedro.
I**'m** from Uruguay.
I**'m not** from Türkiye.

Affirmative	Negative
I'm →	I'm not
You're →	You aren't
He/She's →	He/She isn't
It's →	It isn't
We/They're →	We/They aren't

3 Read the facts and number the pictures.

1. I'm seven.
2. She's my sister.
3. They're on vacation.
4. They aren't my shoes.
5. He isn't happy.
6. Your mom's here!

a
b
c
d  1
e
f

4 Circle the correct option.

Hello, I'm Azra. This is my family. My mom **'s / isn't** next to me. My sister and I **are / aren't** similar. Can you see me? I**'m / 'm not** older than my sister. My grandmother**'s / isn't** in the photo with me, too.

5 Look and complete.

's   'm not   're   'm   ~~isn't~~   aren't

He ___isn't___ old.

They _____ sisters.

I _____ hungry!

I _____ a taxi driver.

We _____ from the U.K.

She _____ seven.

6 Complete these sentences so that they are true for you.

a I _____ six.

b I _____ from Uruguay.

c My best friend _____ a girl.

d My classmates _____ from Mexico.

e My house _____ big.

Grammar: Verb *to be*, Yes/No Questions

Are You My Mommy?

1. Read the story. How many baby ducks are there?

2. Read the story again. Underline the questions in green and the answers in red.

Grammar: Verb *to be*, Yes/No Questions

We use *Yes* or *No* and the verb *to be* to answer some *yes/no* questions.

Yes/No Questions	Short Answers	
Am I a duck?	Yes, you are.	No, you aren't.
Are you my mommy?	Yes, I am.	No, I'm not.
Is he sad?	Yes, he is.	No, he isn't.
Is she happy?	Yes, she is.	No, she isn't.
Is it big?	Yes, it is.	No, it isn't.
Are we a family?	Yes, we are.	No, we aren't.
Are they ostriches?	Yes, they are.	No, they aren't.

3 Read and match the questions with the answers.

1. Is the hill big?
2. Are they my family?
3. Are you ready?
4. Is Big One scared?
5. Are you my mommy?

a. No, I'm not.
b. Yes, he is.
c. Yes, I am.
d. No, it isn't.
e. No, they aren't.

(1 matches d)

4 Unscramble the questions. Check ✓ the correct answer.

a. boy? / he / Is / a _____ Is he a boy? _____

☑ Yes, he is.   ☐ No, he isn't.

b. seven years old? / she / Is _____

☐ Yes, she is.   ☐ No, she isn't.

c. they / cats? / Are _____

☐ Yes, they are.   ☐ No, they aren't.

5) Look and write *Is* or *Are*.

a _____Is_____ Dad hungry? Yes, he is.
b _____ the boys in the tent? Yes, they are.
c _____ Grandma in the house? Yes, she is.
d _____ the little girl happy? No, she isn't.

6) Look again and write the short answers.

a Is it hot? _____No, it isn't._____
b Is the boy's cap blue? _____
c Are the flowers yellow? _____
d Are the boys tired? _____

7) Complete the questions with *Is* or *Are*. Write answers.

a _____Is_____ it sunny today? _____No, it isn't._____
b _____ you six? _____
c _____ you in the classroom? _____
d _____ it the weekend? _____

Learn to Write

Basic Capitalization

We use a capital letter for people's names.

This is **L**uca.

We use a capital letter for the names of countries.

I'm from **M**exico.

1 **Read and number the pictures.**

1. Elif is from Türkiye.
2. Daiyu and Wang Wei are from China.
3. Ms. María is my teacher.
4. My parents' names are Eddie and Lucy.
5. This is my brother Juan.
6. People eat a lot of pasta in Italy.

2 **Underline the names of the people and countries in Activity 1 and write them under the correct heading below.**

Names of People	Names of Countries
Elif	Türkiye

a

b  1

c

d

e

f

Writing

1 **Read about Gabriela and her family.**

My name is Gabriela. I'm seven years old. I'm from Brazil.

My family is big. I live with my parents and two brothers, Lucas and Felipe.

Lucas is three and Felipe is five.

2 **Read the text again and complete the table.**

Name: Gabriela	Age:
Country:	Family size:
Lives with:	Ages:

3 **Look at the table about Haruto and his family.**

Name: Haruto	Age: 6
Country: Japan	Family size: small
Lives with: mom and grandmother	Ages: 32 and 75

4 **Read and complete the text about Haruto using the information in the table.**

My name is _____Haruto_____.

I'm _____ years old.

I'm from _____.

My family is _____.

I live with my _____.

My mom is _____ years old.

5 **Think about you and your family and complete the table.**

Name:	Age:
Country:	Family size:
Lives with:	Ages:

6 **Write and draw about you.**

My name is _____.

I'm _____ years old.

I'm from _____.

My family is _____.

I live with my _____

_____.

My _____

_____ years old.

CHECK

Did you …
- use capital letters for names of people? ☐
- use capital letters for names of countries? ☐

Practice Your Exam Skills

Look at the pictures. Look at the letters. Write the words.

Example

f a m i l y   l-i-f-m-a-y

Questions

1 _____   s-e-u-o-h

2 _____   d-a-b-y-r-c-a-k

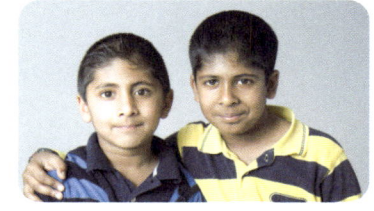

3 _____   r-h-s-b-t-o-r-e

4 _____   e-n-t-t

5 _____   j-a-a-a-m-s-p

2 What is school like?

Grammar: Demonstrative Pronouns: *this, that, these, those*

OAK TREE ELEMENTARY SCHOOL

Home   Class Information   Information for Parents   Trips

Hello, and welcome to your new school!

My name is Mrs. Cook, and I'm the principal.

This is your classroom. Can you see that woman? She's your teacher, Ms. Poole. Those are your classmates.

Most of your classes are in this room. There is a special classroom for art.

This is the cafeteria. These children are eating a healthy lunch.

This is the gym. Those children are doing PE. You can learn lots of new sports at Oak Tree.

See you soon!

1 Read. What can you learn at this school?

2 Circle the correct pronoun in the sentences from the text.

a **(Those)** / **These** are your classmates.

b Can you see **that** / **this** woman?

c **That** / **This** is your classroom.

d **Those** / **These** children are eating a healthy lunch.

e **Those** / **These** children are doing PE.

Grammar: Demonstrative Pronouns: *this*, *that*, *these*, *those*

We use *this*, *that*, *these*, and *those* to show which things we are talking about.
Use *this* and *these* for things near you.
Use *that* and *those* for things far away.

This is the classroom.   **These** are new pencils.   **That** is my teacher.   **Those** are coat racks.

We can use *this*, *that*, *these*, and *those* to ask questions with *be*.

Is **that** your snack?   Are **these** your books?

Spelling Rule
That is ⟶ That's

3 Read and number.
1 This is my classroom.
2 That's the library.
3 These are our lunchboxes.
4 Those are the soccer fields.

a □   b 1   c □   d □

4 Circle the correct words.
a (This) / These is my family.
b These / This are my classmates.
c That / Those is the swimming pool.
d This / These are the bathrooms.

5 **Complete the sentences with *this*, *that*, *these*, or *those*.**

a ___That___ is the music room.
b _____ are my snacks.
c _____ are my brothers.
d _____ is a new pencil case.

6 **Look at the picture and complete the sentences.**

"This is my classroom."

> That is   These are   ~~This is~~   Those are

a ___This is___ Brodie, my best friend.
b _____ the bookshelves.
c _____ my classmates.
d _____ my chair.

Grammar: Possessive Adjectives

Our Class

The students are drawing pictures of their families.

"Your drawings are great!" says Ms. Ellis. "Now let's clean up our classroom!"

Max finds some pencils on the floor. "These aren't my pencils!" he says.

"Look, they're her pencils," says Jake.

Max gives the pencils to Kay.

"Thank you," says Kay.

"Good job! Let's go back to our classroom," says Ms. Ellis.

Jake is sad. He can't find his bag.

"Is this your bag, Jake?" asks Molly.

"Yes, thanks!" says Jake.

Now the class can go.

1 Read. Who can't find his bag?

2 Find these words in the text and underline them in the correct color.

<u>my</u>   <u>your</u>   <u>his</u>   <u>her</u>   <u>our</u>   <u>their</u>

3 Mark ✓ or ✗.

a The students are drawing pictures of their families. ☐

b The students are in their classroom. ☐

c Jake can't find his bag. ☐

Grammar: Possessive Adjectives

We use possessive adjectives to talk about a relationship with a person.
My best friend is Amelia.
We use possessive adjectives to say who owns something.
Her bag is pink.

I	**My** grandmother is very old.
You	**Your** lunchbox is new.
He	**His** books are on the table.
She	**Her** brothers are tall.
We	**Our** cousins live in an apartment.
They	**Their** drawings are on the wall.

4 Circle the correct words.

a I have one brother. **His / Her** name is Felipe.

b This is my aunt. **His / Her** name is Ellie.

c The students are very noisy. **Their / His** teacher isn't happy.

5 Look and complete.

his   her   your   our   ~~my~~   their

a This is ___my___ new bag.

b The students finished _____ drawings.

c My mom is a nurse. _____ job is interesting.

d _____ school isn't big.

e My uncle lives in Japan. _____ apartment is small.

f Is _____ name Tom?

6 Unscramble and complete the sentences. Then, match them with the pictures.

1. is / Her — _Her_ bag _is_ colorful.
2. tall / His / is — _____ sister _____.
3. Our / are / new — _____ tablets _____.
4. house / Their / big — _____ isn't _____.
5. is / My / new — _____ book _____.
6. is / Our — _____ teacher _____ nice.

7 Unscramble and rewrite the sentences.

a. teacher / nice / His / is

b. is / book / new / Their

Learn to Write

Question Marks

We use question marks at the end of a question.
- **What's your name?**
- **Is this your coat?**

Questions start with a capital letter, too.
- **Where's my classroom?**
- **Are these your pens?**

1 Write a period or a question mark.

a Is he your cousin [?]

b This is my tent [ ]

c Where are your parents [ ]

d Are these your shoes [ ]

e What's his name [ ]

f I live near my school [ ]

2 Unscramble and complete the questions.

a is / Where / the

_____ Where is the _____ music room?

b from / are / you

Where _____?

c teacher / new / Is

_____ your _____?

d How / brother?

_____ old is your _____

e lab / Is / big

_____ the computer _____?

f Do / school / you

_____ have lunch at _____?

Writing

1 Read Alex's conversation with a new student and underline the questions.

Hello. I'm Alex. What's your name?

My name's Marco.

Welcome, Marco! This is our classroom, and those are the soccer fields. Do you like playing soccer?

Yes, I do.

Great. Me, too!

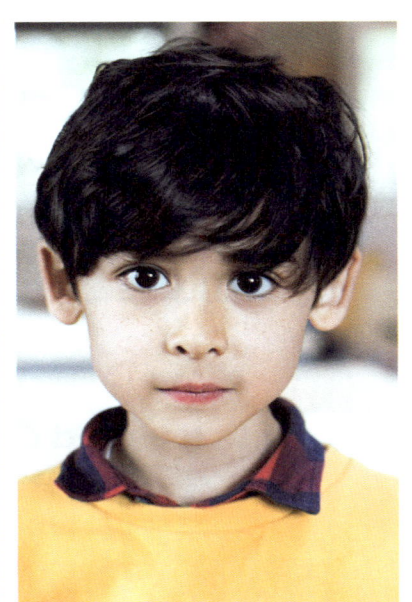

2 Read the conversation again and complete the questions.

a _____ hat's your name _____

b _____ o you like playing soccer _____

3 Read Sofía's conversation with a new student and underline the questions.

Hello, María! Welcome to our school. Where are you from?

I'm from Mexico.

This is our classroom, and that's the art room. Do you like drawing?

Yes, I do.

Great. Me, too!

4 Look at the questions Sofía asks in Activity 3 and circle the correct options.

a **What / Where** are you from **! / ?**

b **Do / do** you like drawing **? / .**

5 Draw yourself and a new student at school. Complete the conversation.

Hello. Welcome to our school. _____ your name?

_____

_____ are you from _____

I'm _____.

_____ you like the new school?

_____

CHECK

Did you ...
• start questions with a capital letter? ☐
• end questions with a question mark? ☐

21

Practice Your Exam Skills

Look and read. Mark ✓ or X.
Examples

 This is a bag. ✓

 This is a book. X

1  This is a tent. ☐

2  These are snacks. ☐

3  This is a computer lab. ☐

4  This is a coat rack. ☐

5  These are desks. ☐

3 What are living things?

Grammar: *There is, there are*

Hilltop Nature Park

Dear Grandma,

I'm on a school trip. We're at Hilltop Nature Park. There is a big lake here. There are fish and frogs in the lake. There are lots of water lilies, too. We're fishing with our nets. It's fun!

After lunch, we're looking for birds. There are birds on the lake and in the trees. There is a small hut for watching birds.

See you soon!

Love, Alfie

1. Read the postcard. What is Alfie doing after lunch?

2. Underline the sentences with *There is* in blue and the sentences with *There are* in red.

3. Circle *There is* or *There are*.
   a **There is** / **There are** a big lake.
   b **There is** / **There are** fish and frogs in the lake.
   c **There is** / **There are** lots of water lilies, too.
   d **There is** / **There are** a small hut for watching birds.

Grammar: *There is, there are*

We use *there is* and *there are* to say how many things are around us.

There is a frog.

There are flowers in the garden.

Spelling Rule
There is ⟶ There's

4 Look at the pictures and write *1* or *2*.

a There are tall trees. `1`
b There is a water lily on the pond. ☐
c There is an apple tree. ☐
d There are tomato plants. ☐
e There are sunflowers. ☐
f There is a bird in the tree. ☐

5 **Look at the picture and complete the sentences with *There is* or *There are*.**

a _____*There are*_____ blue flowers in the forest.
b _____ some fish in the stream.
c _____ yellow flowers next to the stream.
d _____ two children looking at a fishing net.
e _____ a parent looking at a bird.
f _____ a hill.

6 **Write three sentences about the living things you can see or imagine.**

a There's a _____.
b There are _____.
c There are _____.

Grammar: Prepositions of Place: *in, on, under, next to*

HOW TO MAKE A BUG HOTEL

Ladybugs and other insects will be happy in this easy-to-make bug hotel!

You need:
- strong cardboard tubes or old plant pots (or recycle clean coffee cups!)
- dry plant stems
- pine cones
- twigs and leaves
- string

How to make:

1 Put the plant stems, pine cones, twigs, and leaves in the tubes or plant pots.

2 Put the tubes next to some flowers, or put them under lots of leaves.

3 Or, hang pots in a low tree.

1 Read. What can you put in a bug hotel?

2 Read again and find these sentences. Complete them with the missing words.

a Put them _____under_____ lots of leaves.

b Hang pots _____ a low tree.

c Put twigs and leaves _____ the tubes.

d Put the tubes _____ some flowers.

3 Circle the correct words.

a Flowers can grow **in / next to** the bug hotel.

b Dragonflies stay **under / on** the water.

c Fish live **in / next to** a pond.

Grammar: Prepositions of Place: *in, on, under, next to*

We use *in, on, under,* and *next to* to talk about where something is.

Where is the earthworm? It's **in** the soil.

Where are the bees? They're **on** the flowers.

Where is the lizard? It's **under** the rock.

Where are the frogs? They're **next to** the pond.

4 Read and number.

1  2  3  4

a The water lily is on the pond. ☐ b The birds are in the tree. ☐
c The ducks are under the bridge. ☐ d The spider is next to the wasp. ☐

(b is marked 2)

5 Unscramble and complete the sentences.

a on / My / is

___My___ bug hotel ___is on___ the tree branch.

b There / in / are

_____ mosquitoes _____ the backyard.

c a / I / under

_____ see _____ mouse _____ the flower.

d is / There / next to

_____ a forest _____ the pond.

6 Look at the picture and complete with *in*, *on*, *under*, or *next to*.

a   Where's the cat? _____On_____ the chair.
b   Where's the lettuce? _____ the tomatoes.
c   Where are the roses? _____ the tree.
d   Where are the drinks? _____ the table.
e   Where's the boy? _____ the tree.
f   Where's the hat? _____ the fence.

7 Draw a garden and hide things in it. Match the words with where the things are.

in

on

under

next to

Learn to Write

Commas

We use a comma (,) after each word in a list.

I like mangoes, apples, and corn.

We grow tulips, sunflowers, and roses.

1 Circle the commas in the sentences.
   a Earthworms, ants, and beetles live underground.
   b I have milk, bread, and cheese for breakfast.
   c We walked to the pond, the playground, and the forest this morning.
   d I like rabbits, dolphins, ladybugs, and butterflies.

2 Add commas to the sentences.

   a Apples, pears, and bananas grow on trees.
   b Dragonflies spiders and ladybugs eat other insects.
   c My sister brother and cousin all go to the same school.
   d Tomatoes peas and corn grow on plants.
   e The gym the music room and the art room are in a different building.

Writing

1 Read about the garden in Elif's school.

Our School Garden

In our school garden, there are lots of flowers. There are roses, marigolds, and sunflowers in summer. We grow lettuce, tomatoes, and peas. Sometimes, we can eat these vegetables! There are lots of insects, too. My class helps in the garden on Tuesdays. It's really fun!

2 Read the text again and underline the plants in green and the animals in red.

3 Cross out the words that don't belong to the groups.

Plants	Animals
rose	tomato
mosquito	frog
water lily	fish
sunflower	ant
bee	marigold

4 Draw a backyard with plants and animals.

5 Write about the backyard you drew in Activity 4. Don't forget to use commas.

My Backyard

In my backyard, there are _____
_____
_____ .

There are _____
_____
_____ , too.

I love my backyard!

CHECK

Did you … • use commas correctly? ☐

Practice Your Exam Skills

Look and read. Write *yes* or *no*.

Examples

There are two bees on the purple flowers.	yes
The boy is playing with the puppet.	no

Questions

1 The tomato plants are tall.

2 There are some toy cars under a chair.

3 There is a dragonfly in the picture.

4 There is a drink on the table.

5 The helicopter is red.

4 What is a friend?

Grammar: Present Simple: Affirmative and Negative

Hi! I'm Max.

On Tuesdays and Wednesdays, my mom works. On those days, I go to an after-school program. It's called Happy Days. It's next to my school.

My best friend doesn't go to Happy Days, but I have good friends there. We play soccer and basketball outside. Sometimes we help each other with our homework, and we share snacks.

My sister, Bella, goes to Happy Days, too. She draws pictures, and she makes things. I don't play with her because she always plays with her friends.

I like Tuesdays and Wednesdays!

1 Read. When does Max go to Happy Days?

2 Read again and circle *True* or *False*.
- a Max's mom doesn't work. True (False)
- b Max has some good friends at Happy Days. True False
- c Max rides a bike at Happy Days. True False
- d Bella reads stories at Happy Days. True False

33

Grammar: Present Simple: Affirmative and Negative

We use the present simple to talk about facts and routines.
We make negative statements in the simple present with *don't* and *doesn't*.

Affirmative	Negative
I go to an after-school program.	I don't go home after school.
You walk to school.	You don't walk home.
She plays with her friends. He plays soccer.	She doesn't play with me. He doesn't play basketball.
We share snacks.	We don't share our dinner.
They ride bikes in the park.	They don't ride bikes to school.

3 Circle the correct words. Then, number the pictures.

After school …

1. I **go** / **goes** to the park with my friend.
2. He **go** / **goes** home. He helps his mom.
3. We **doesn't** / **don't** walk home. We ride our bikes.
4. She **doesn't** / **don't** go home. She visits her grandmother.

a

b 1

c

d

4 Match to make sentences.

a I
b He
c We
d She

1 plays with her friends.
2 go roller-blading in the park.
3 live next to my best friend.
4 doesn't go to my school.

5 Complete. Use the correct form of the verbs.

a **watch:** I ____don't watch____ ✗ TV with my friends.
I ____watch____ ✓ TV with my sister.

b **fly:** We _____ ✓ kites in the park.
We _____ ✗ kites near the trees.

c **play:** He _____ ✗ computer games at night.
He _____ ✓ them in the morning.

d **draw:** My sister _____ ✓ lots of pictures,
but she _____ ✗ pictures for me!

6 Complete. Use the correct form of the verbs.

> read   live   climb   go   ~~visit~~   sleep

a During the summer break,
I ____visit____ my cousin.

b My cousin _____
near me. We fly to his house.

c We _____ to
the movies. We play outside.

d We _____ trees,
and we play in the tree house.

e At night, we _____
in a tent in the backyard.

f In the tent, my cousin
_____ scary stories!

Grammar: Present Simple: *Yes/No* Questions

PETS' CORNER

Gemma has two rabbits. Gemma, tell us about them, please!

My rabbits are Blackie and Bobby. Blackie is the black one!

Do you take care of your rabbits?
Yes, I do. I feed them every day. I give them water, too.

Do you have a favorite?
Yes, I do. Blackie is my favorite. She's small and fast. My sister likes Bobby. He's easier to hold.

Does your sister help take care of the rabbits?
No, she doesn't. She's too young.

Do the rabbits play together?
Yes, they do. They're good friends. Blackie chases Bobby, but I think Bobby likes that!

Do you play with Blackie?
Yes, I do. I give Blackie some boxes, and we play Hide-and-Seek. She likes boxes.

1 Read the interview. What are the names of Gemma's rabbits?

2 Read the interview again. Underline the questions in blue.

3 Read and match.

1. Does Gemma have two rabbits?
2. Does Gemma's sister feed the rabbits?
3. Do the rabbits play together?
4. Does Blackie like boxes?
5. Does Bobby chase Blackie?

a. Yes, they do.
b. No, he doesn't.
c. No, she doesn't.
d. Yes, she does.
e. Yes, she does.

Grammar: Present Simple: *Yes/No* Questions

We make *yes/no* questions using *Do* and *Does*.

Do you play with Blackie?   **Does** Blackie like boxes?

We can answer with *Yes + do / does* or *No + don't / doesn't*.

Yes, I **do**.   Yes, she **does**.
No, I **don't**.   No, she **doesn't**.

Question	Affirmative Short Answer	Negative Short Answer
Do you **live** near school?	Yes, I **do**.	No, I **don't**.
Does he **play** games?	Yes, he **does**.	No, he **doesn't**.
Does she **play** games?	Yes, she **does**.	No, she **doesn't**.
Do rabbits **run** fast?	Yes, they **do**.	No, they **don't**.

4 Check ✓ the correct questions. Cross out ✗ the incorrect questions and write the correct word.

a Does you play soccer? ✗ _Do you play soccer?_

b Do your best friend live near you? ☐ _____

c Do you play with friends? ☐ _____

d Do your friends like basketball? ☐ _____

e Do your school have a computer lab? ☐ _____

5 Circle the correct words.

a Do you have a pencil sharpener?
   Yes, I **(do)** / **does**.

b Do you have a music room at your school?
   Yes, we **do** / **does**.

c Do you wear a uniform at your school?
   No, I **don't** / **doesn't**.

d Does your best friend like English?
   No, he **don't** / **doesn't**.

6 Look at the picture and complete the answers.

a	Do Mia and Jess wear glasses?	Yes, _they do_ .
b	Does Mia have short hair?	No, _____ .
c	Do Mia and Jess wear a uniform?	Yes, _____ .
d	Does Jess play tennis?	No, _____ .
e	Do they ride bikes to school?	No, _____ .

7 Complete the questions. Then, write answers for you.

a _Do_ you like school?
   Yes, I do.

b _____ you draw pictures?
   _____

c _____ your parents draw pictures?
   _____

d _____ your teacher ride a bike to school?
   _____

Learn to Write

Capital Letters and Periods

We start a new sentence with a capital letter. The sentences can end with a period.

He is my best friend.

There is a water lily in the pond.

1 **Underline the capital letters in red and underline the periods in green.**

a <u>M</u>y friend helps me with homework<u>.</u>

b On Fridays, I go to art class.

c Charlie draws pictures of dragonflies.

d Mom and Dad both work, and I go to an after-school program.

2 **Rewrite the sentences. Use capital letters and periods.**

a my sister is a good friend

<u>My sister is a good friend.</u>

b we go roller-blading together

_____

c she reads stories to me

_____

d we share our toys

_____

e we walk together to school

_____

Writing

My best friend is Gus.
He is seven years old.
We play Hide-and-Seek together at recess.
We eat our lunch together.
Gus likes soccer.

My best friend is Emma.
She is six years old.
We share snacks at recess.
We play on the swings together.
Emma likes art.

1 Read the texts and complete the table.

Name of Best Friend:	Gus	Emma
Age:		
Do Together:		
Do Together:		
Likes:		

2 Think about your best friend. Complete the table.

Name of Best Friend:	
Age:	
Do Together:	
Do Together:	
Likes:	

3 Use the information from Activity 2 to write about your best friend. Then, draw him/her.

My best friend _____ .

_____ is _____

years _____ .

We _____

_____

_____ .

_____ likes _____ .

CHECK

Did you ...
- use a capital letter at the beginning of sentences? ☐
- use a period at the end of sentences? ☐

Practice Your Exam Skills

Read. Choose a word from the box. Write the correct word next to the numbers 1–5. There is one example.

The Park

There's a park near my _____house_____. I like this park. It's very big. I go to the park with my best friend Felix. He lives near me. We go to the park after 1 _____. We ride our 2 _____ there. At the park, there are swings and a 3 _____. But I like the jungle gym the most. Sometimes other 4 _____ come to the park, and we all play 5 _____ together. Then, we have something to drink and share snacks.

Example

house   soccer   books   bikes

school   teacher   slide   children

5 How do we have fun?

Billy

Grammar: Present Simple: *like, likes, don't like, doesn't like*

Summer Fun

We have a long summer break. It's lots of fun. I like going to the beach with my family. We like playing games on the beach. I like swimming in the ocean. My sister doesn't like swimming. She likes playing mini-golf and basketball with her friends.

Winter break is shorter, and it's cold then. I don't like going outside. My sister and I like baking cookies together. I like playing with my toy cars. I have a big collection of cars. My sister likes dancing to music.

1 Read. What do Billy and his sister like doing together?

2 Read and write *Yes* or *No*.

a Billy likes going to the beach with his family.   Yes

b Billy likes swimming in the ocean.   _____

c Billy's sister likes swimming in the ocean, too.   _____

d Billy likes going outside in the winter.   _____

e Billy and his sister have a long summer break.   _____

f Billy's sister likes dancing.   _____

Grammar: Present Simple: *like, likes, don't like, doesn't like*

We use *like* and *likes* with verb + *ing* to talk about the things we enjoy.

We use *don't like* and *doesn't like* with verb + *ing* to talk about the things we don't enjoy.

Affirmative	Negative
I like playing board games.	I don't like reading.
You like making presents.	You don't like shopping.
He likes playing with toy cars. She likes collecting comics.	He doesn't like dancing. She doesn't like collecting dolls.
We like baking cookies.	We don't like jumping rope.
They like roller-blading.	They don't like riding bikes.

Spelling Rules

fly → flying
dance → dancing
bake → baking
swim → swimming
run → running

3 Read the sentences and draw ☺ or ☹ in the table below.

a Alice likes jumping rope.
b Hugo and Tom don't like painting.
c Alice doesn't like riding a bike.
d Alice likes painting.
e Hugo and Tom don't like jumping rope.
f Hugo and Tom like riding bikes.

	🪢	🎨	🚲
Alice	☺	☺	☺
Hugo and Tom	☺	☺	☺

4) **Circle the correct words.**
   a He **doesn't like** / **don't like** going to the park.
   b I **likes** / **like** drawing pictures.
   c We **like** / **likes** traveling by plane.
   d They **don't like** / **doesn't like** writing stories

5) **Look and complete the sentences with** *like*, *likes*, *don't like*, **or** *doesn't like*.

They ____like____ playing board games.

He _____ walking in the rain.

We _____ playing catch.

You _____ tying your shoelaces.

She _____ making birthday cards.

I _____ sleeping in a tent.

6) **Draw one of your best friends and complete the sentences about him/her.**

   a My friend likes _____.

   b My friend doesn't like _____.

45

Grammar: Possessive 's

Where Is Max's Train?

Max likes playing with his train. Max's train is red, yellow, and blue.

Today, Max can't find his train.

Max picks up the toys.

But it isn't. It's Ava's doll.

But it isn't. It's Dad's hat.

1 Read. Where is Max's train?

2 Read and write *Yes* or *No*.

   a   Max's train is red, yellow, and green.   ___No___

   b   Ava's doll is red, yellow, and blue.   _____

   c   Max's dad is wearing his hat.   _____

   d   Max's sister is playing with her doll.   _____

46

Grammar: Possessive 's

We add 's to the end of a name to show who something belongs to.

This is Lou's teddy bear.

These are Dan's parents.

Sam and Matt's tent is green.

3 Read and match. Then, underline the possessive 's in each sentence.

1 My dad's car is green.
2 Lucy's hair is very long.
3 Sam and Anna's house is next to the school.
4 My brother's soccer ball is black and gray.

a
b
c
d  `1`

4 Read and check ✓ the correct sentence.

a May's ball is in the backyard.
Mays ball is in the backyard.

b Pablos bike is red.
Pablo's bike is red.

c My brothers kite is old.
My brother's kite is old.

d My moms cookies are very big.
My mom's cookies are very big.

a
b
c
d

5 Follow the lines and write.

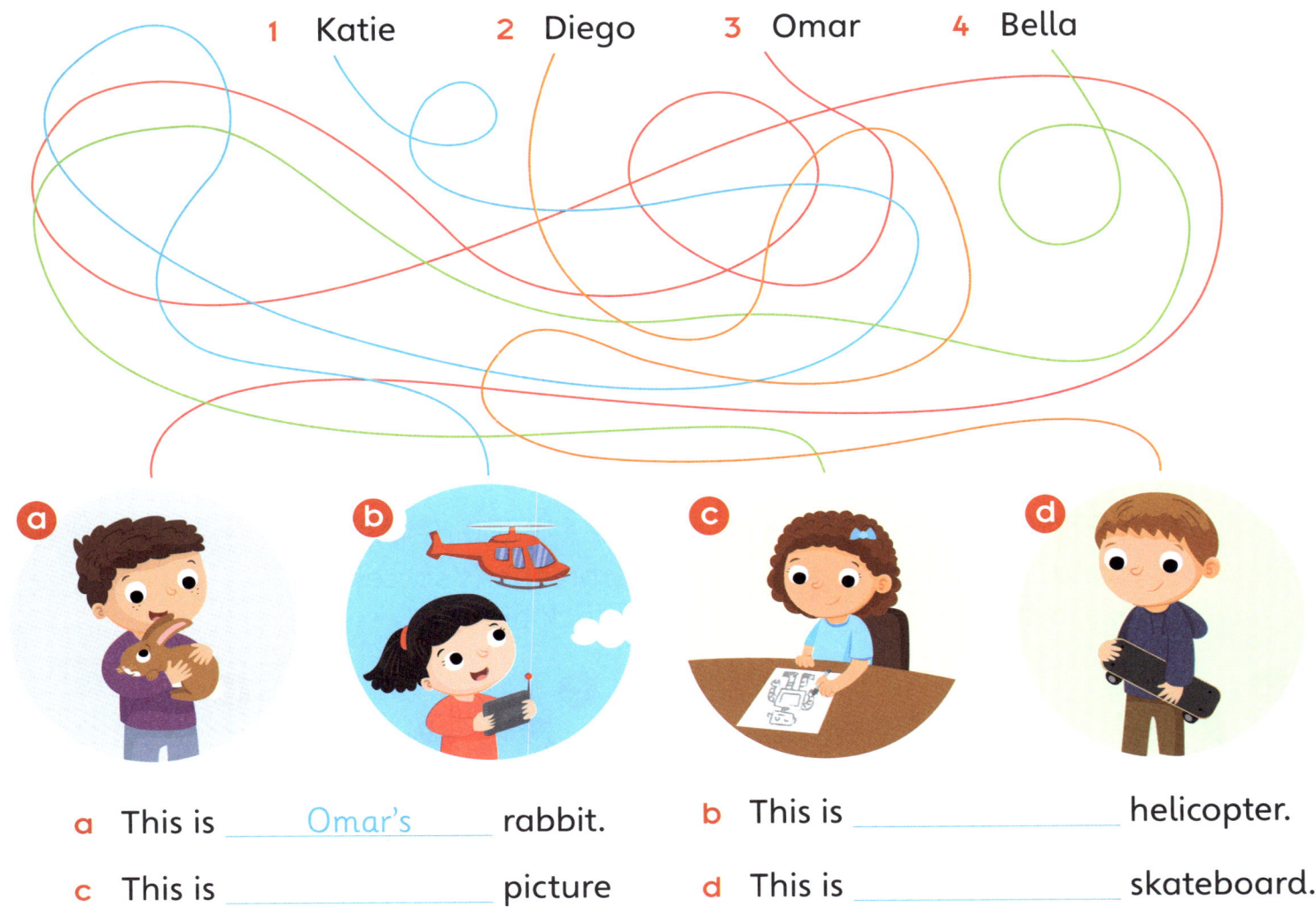

1 Katie   2 Diego   3 Omar   4 Bella

a This is ___Omar's___ rabbit.
b This is _____ helicopter.
c This is _____ picture.
d This is _____ skateboard.

6 Write sentences using the words below.

Connor / yo-yo / red — Connor's yo-yo is red.

Roberto / parents / on vacation — Roberto's parents are on vacation.

a Toby / helicopter / new
b Rosy / dollhouse / big
c Donna / cousins / twins
d Lily / building blocks / colorful

Learn to Write

Exclamation Points

We use an exclamation point to show strong feelings or surprise.

I don't like getting up on Mondays!

People in Indonesia like eating dragonflies!

1 Underline the exclamations points in the sentences.
   a Snails can sleep for three years!
   b I eat apples at lunch.
   c Do you want to go the park?
   d I can swim underwater for 15 meters!
   e Do you like playing mini-golf?
   f This peanut butter is delicious!

2 Complete the sentences with a period (.), a question mark (?), or an exclamation point (!).
   a I love visiting my cousins during the summer break !
   b Don't litter in the park ☐
   c Do you want fries or rice ☐
   d I walk to school ☐
   e What's your favorite board game ☐

Writing

1 Read and underline what Ella and Lucas like doing during summer break.

My Summer Break

During summer break, I like playing with my friends at the park. I can walk to three parks from my house! I like listening to music, too.

Sometimes my family goes to the ocean. We like sailing a boat on the ocean. It's a lot of fun!

Ella

My Summer Break

During summer break, I like riding my bike with my brother. I like playing video games, too. I have 15 different games!

Sometimes my family goes to a theme park. I like going on the rides. But the tallest ride is too scary for me!

Lucas

2 Read the sentences that show the children's strong feelings or surprise. Write E for Ella and L for Lucas.

a I have 15 different games! ☐

b I can walk to three parks from my house! ☐

c It's a lot of fun! ☐

d But the tallest ride is too scary for me! ☐

3 Write what you and your family like doing during your summer break.

a I like _____.

b I like _____.

c We like _____.

4 Write about your summer break using your ideas from Activity 3. Add one or two sentences that show a strong feeling or surprise.

During summer break, I like _____

I like _____, too.

Sometimes my family goes to _____

We like _____

_____

5 Draw a picture of your summer break.

CHECK

Did you ...
- write a sentence showing a strong feeling? ☐
- write a sentence showing something surprising? ☐
- use exclamation points in the correct place? ☐

Practice Your Exam Skills

Look at the pictures and read the questions. Write one word to answer.

Example
What's the girl doing? Listening to _____music_____.

Questions
1 How many people are in the car? _____.

2 Where are the children? On a _____.
3 What's the mom eating? An _____ cream cone.

4 What are they doing? Playing _____.
5 What color is the boy's hat? _____.

6 How can we help?

Grammar: Present Simple: *have/has*, Affirmative and Negative

The Lakes Animal Shelter Needs You!

The Lakes Animal Shelter has over 40 animals that need a new home.

"I like animals. I have some free time. I like helping."

Please think about adopting one of our furry friends!

We have lots of photos of our animals on our website.

If you don't have space or time for a pet, you can still help us!

- Donate blankets and pet food.
- Help walk the dogs.
- Help brush and feed the animals.

We have a visitors' day every month. Come and see what we do!

1 Read. Where can you find photos of the animals?

2 Read again and circle *has* or *have*.

a It **(has)** / **have** over 40 animals.

b I **has** / **have** some free time.

c We **has** / **have** lots of photos of our animals.

d If you don't **has** / **have** space or time for a pet …

e We **has** / **have** a visitors' day every month.

53

Grammar: Present Simple: *have/has*, Affirmative and Negative

We use *have* and *has* to talk about things that do and don't belong to us and tasks we do or don't have to do.

I **have** a pet.

We **don't have** cans to recycle.

He **has** homework today.

She **doesn't have** homework today.

Affirmative	Negative
I have a sister.	I don't have a brother.
You have two brothers.	You don't have chores on Fridays.
He has a bike.	She doesn't have a water bottle.
We have a birdfeeder in the backyard.	We don't have a backyard.
They have a lot of homework.	They don't have math today.

3 Look at the pictures and mark ✓ the correct sentence.

a

1 It doesn't have food. ☐
2 It has food. ✓

b

1 They don't have blond hair. ☐
2 They have blond hair. ☐

c

1 He has bottles to recycle. ☐
2 He has cans to recycle. ☐

d

1 I have a lot of toys. ☐
2 I don't have a lot of toys. ☐

4. **Look at the picture and complete the sentences with *has*, *doesn't have*, *have*, or *don't have*.**

a They ____have____ a lot of bottles for their game.

b She _____ a pen.

c She _____ bag of books.

d He _____ a book.

e They _____ lemonade.

f He _____ some coins.

5. **Look at picture *a* and complete. Then, write two sentences about picture *b*.**

She doesn't ____have____ rabbits.

She _____ mice.

The mice _____ a wheel.

Grammar: Present Simple: Wh-questions with have / has

The Shopping List

Sylvie: What do you have on the shopping list, Grandpa?

Grandpa: I have apples and bread on my list. What else do I need?

Sylvie: What do you have in the fridge?

Grandpa: Let's look.

Sylvie: Look, Grandpa. You have butter and chicken. You don't have milk. Put milk on the list.

Grandpa: OK.

Sylvie: What else do you have on the shopping list, Grandpa?

Grandpa: I have potatoes and peas on my list.

Sylvie: Oh, Grandpa! You have a lot of potatoes. Don't put potatoes on the list!

1 **Read. Where are Grandpa and Sylvie?**

2 **Read and write the answers.**

   a What does Grandpa have on his shopping list at the end? _____

   b What does Grandpa have in his fridge? _____

Grammar: Present Simple: *Wh*-questions with *have / has*

We can make questions using *What*, *do/does*, and *have*.

What do you **have** in your bag?
I **have** a pencil case and a notebook.

What does Grandma **have** in the fridge?
She **has** eggs and water.

3 Read and match. Then, underline *do* and *does* in the questions.

1  What do they have?

a  They have tennis rackets.

2  What does she have?

b  They have a helicopter and a plane.

3  What does he have?

c  She has a teddy bear.

4  What do they have?

d  He has a skateboard.

4 Read and circle the correct words.

a What **do** / **(does)** the girl have? She has a pitcher of water.
b What **do** / **does** the boys have? They have knives and forks.
c What **do** / **does** Dad have? He has a chicken.

5. **Unscramble and complete the questions. Then, number the pictures.**

1. he / have / does
   What _____does he have_____ in his bag?

2. she / have / does
   What _____ in her bag?

3. do / they / have
   What _____ in their bags?

6. **Complete the questions. Then, match.**

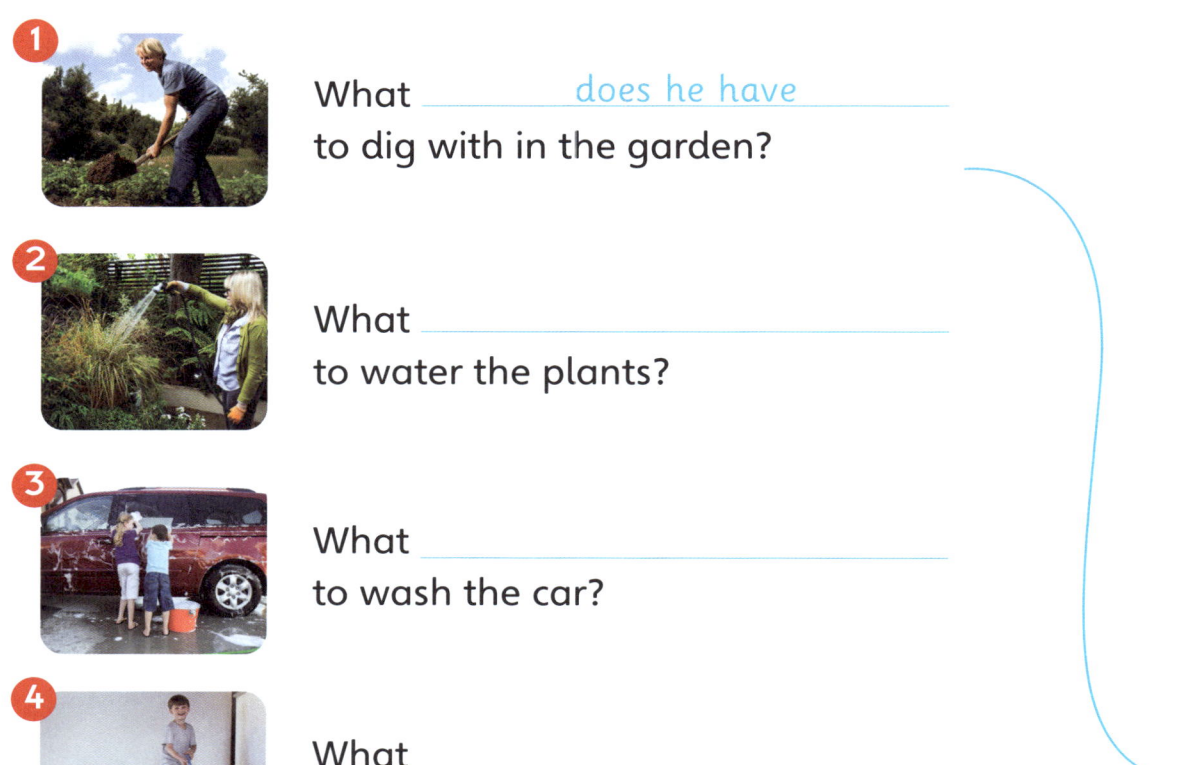

1. What _____does he have_____ to dig with in the garden?

2. What _____ to water the plants?

3. What _____ to wash the car?

4. What _____ to sweep the floor?

Learn to Write

Nouns

A noun can be a person, an animal, a place, or a thing.

My sister sets the table.   **Birds fly to hot countries.**
   (person)   (thing)   (animal)   (place)

1 Underline the nouns. Use different colors.

____ = person   ____ = animal
____ = place   ____ = thing

a Mom hangs our clothes to dry.
b The wind is strong, and the clothes dry.
c Our cat plays in the wind.
d My brother can fly his kite on the hill.

2 Write the nouns from the box that go with each sentence.

birds   ~~vet~~   bed   countryside   animal shelter   books

a The (person) helps the cat.

_____vet_____

b I buy food online because I live in the (place).

_____

c We donate our old (things) to the library.

_____

d Put out water for (animals) in the summer.

_____

e You can adopt a pet from the (place).

_____

f I make my (thing) every day.

_____

Writing

1 Read how Jamie helps others. Then, complete the mind map.

How I Can Help Others

There are lots of ways we can help others.
Every morning, I make my bed.
My sister and I set the table for dinner.
Sometimes, I water the plants.
I make cookies for my friends when they are sad.

How I Can Help Others

make my bed

2 Read about how Faye helps others. Then, complete the text.

How I Can Help Others

There are lots of ways we can help others.
I  take out the recycling at home.
Every morning, I  _____
On weekends, I go to the supermarket with my grandma and
 _____
Sometimes, my brother and I
_____ in the park.

3) **Think about how you help others. Complete the mind map with pictures and words.**

How I Can Help Others

4) **Write about how you help others. Use your ideas from Activity 3.**

_____

There are lots of ways we can help others. I _____

_____

Every morning, I _____

On weekends, I _____

Sometimes, I _____

5) **Choose one of the ideas you wrote about and draw yourself doing it.**

CHECK

Did you ... • use nouns in sentences? ☐

61

Practice Your Exam Skills

Look at the pictures. Look at the letters. Write the words.

Example

b o x e s   x-e-b-s-o

Questions

1    _____   r-a-t-h-s

2    _____   e-k-b-r-a

3    _____   s-i-t-l

4    _____   e-g-i-a-r-g-d-n-n

5    _____   y-d-i-t

7 Why do we need plants and animals?

Grammar: *Can, can't*

HONEYBEES

They eat pollen and drink nectar from flowers. Bees can make honey from nectar.

Bees help plants. They carry pollen from plant to plant. Plants use the pollen to grow more plants.

Bees don't fly in winter. They stay in their hive and eat honey.

Honey bees live in big groups in a hive. Bees can fly very fast, but they can't fly as fast as dragonflies. They can beat their wings 200 times a second. Bees can see many colors, but they can't see red.

1. **Read. How do bees help plants?**

2. **Read and complete the table.**

What can bees do?	What can't bees do?
fly very fast	

Grammar: Can, can't

We use *can* to talk about things we are able to do.

I can ride a bike. **Bees can fly.**

We use *can't* to talk about things we are not able to do.

She can't read. **It can't swim.**

Affirmative	Negative
I can play soccer.	I can't play tennis.
You can run fast.	You can't roller-skate.
He can climb trees.	He can't ride a bike.
She can catch.	She can't jump rope.
It can make honey.	A rabbit can't fly
We can bake cookies.	We can't see well at night.
They can walk on ice.	Bees can't swim.

3 Read and circle the correct words. Then, number the pictures.

a Bats **can** / **can't** sleep upside down.

b An elephant **can** / **can't** jump.

c Cows **can** / **can't** swim.

d A hippo **can** / **can't** climb a tree.

e Giraffes **can** / **can't** run fast.

1

4 Complete the sentences with *can* or *can't*.

a Frogs ____can____ swim.
b Frogs _____ live on land and in water.
c Frogs _____ fly.
d Frogs _____ jump.
e Frogs _____ sing.
f Frogs _____ bake cookies.

5 Look and complete the sentences with *can* or *can't* and a word from the box.

paint   ~~catch~~   skateboard   bake   dance   jump

a He ____can't catch____ .
b She _____ rope.
c They _____ well.
d He _____.
e She _____ pictures.
f He _____ cookies.

6 Write one sentence about what you can do and one sentence about what you can't do. Use the words from Activity 5.

I can dance. I can't bake cookies.

_____

65

Grammar: Countable and Uncountable Nouns

1 Read and number the pictures.

What am I?

1 I eat everything. I can give you some milk. I can climb high. What am I?

2 I live in a cold country. I have two wings. But I can't fly. What am I?

3 I love purple flowers. I can make you some honey. I live in a hive. What am I?

4 I live in some soil. I'm good for the plants. I can't see. What am I?

☐

1

☐

☐

2 Read and complete the table with the countable and uncountable nouns.

~~some milk~~   ~~a country~~   two wings   flowers
some honey   a hive   some soil   the plants

Countable	Uncountable
a country	some milk

66

Grammar: Countable and Uncountable Nouns

For nouns that we can count:
We use *a* when there is only one.
   This is a flower.
We add *s* when there is more than one.
   There are two bees.

For nouns that we can't count:
We use *some* before the noun. We don't add *s* at the end.
   There is some water in the glass.

3 Read and write *1* or *2*. Then, underline all the countable nouns.

1

2

a   There are many sandwiches.   `1`
b   There is some juice.   ☐
c   There is a banana.   ☐
d   There is some water.   ☐
e   There is some cheese.   ☐
f   There are six eggs.   ☐

67

4 Look at the picture and complete the sentences using *There is* or *There are*.

a _____There is_____ a watermelon.
b _____ three flowers.
c _____ some milk.
d _____ a big cake.
e _____ many cookies.
f _____ a candle.

5 Look at the picture and complete the sentences with *a* or *some*.

a There are _____ apple trees.
b There is _____ hive.
c There is _____ honey in the hive.
d There is _____ water in the pond.

6 Look at the picture in Activity 5 to write some more sentence. Use the words provided.

a _____There is some bread._____ (some bread)
b _____ (two frogs)
c _____ (a cave)
d _____ (some juice)
e _____ (two hills)

Learn to Write

Verbs

We use verbs to talk about actions.
A bat eats fruit. A bat wakes up at night.
We use verbs to talk about a state of being.
Bats have fur. They are mammals.

1 **Underline the verbs.**
   a Octopuses <u>live</u> in the ocean.
   b They have a hard beak.
   c Octopuses eat crabs and shellfish.
   d They build homes with rocks.
   e They are very smart!

2 **Complete the sentences using the verbs in the box.**

   have   ~~push~~   climb   live   plant   breathe

   a Reindeer _____ push _____ snow with their antlers.
   b Farmers usually _____ crops in the spring.
   c Some goats _____ trees.
   d Frogs _____ through their skin and their mouth.
   e Butterflies only _____ for a few weeks.
   f Octopuses _____ eight arms.

Writing

1. Read about kangaroos.

Amazing Animals: Kangaroos

Kangaroos live in Australia. They have strong back legs. They can jump more than nine meters high!

Kangaroos eat grass and different kinds of leaves.

Baby kangaroos are three centimeters long when they are born. Mothers carry their babies in a pouch.

2. Make notes about kangaroos.

Where do they live?	Australia
Description (have/are):	have strong back legs
What do they eat?	
Amazing facts:	

3. Look at the notes. Use them to complete the text about blue whales.

Where do they live?	all five oceans
Description (have/are):	are 30 meters long
What do they eat?	fish
Amazing facts:	talk to each other

Amazing Animals: Blue Whales

Blue whales live in _____all five oceans_____.

They _____.

That's the same as two buses. They eat _____.

Blue whales can _____.

4 **Think about an amazing animal. Write notes about it and draw a picture of it.**

Where do they live?	
Description (have/are):	
What do they eat?	
Amazing facts:	

5 **Write about your amazing animal using your notes above.**

_____

_____ live _____

They _____

They eat _____

They _____

_____

CHECK

Did you ... • write sentences using verbs? ☐

Practice Your Exam Skills

Look and read. Put a check ✓ or an ✗ in the box. There are two examples.

Examples

 This is a table cloth. ✓

 These are penguins. ✗

1  These are eggs. ☐

2  This is a hive. ☐

3  This is a forest. ☐

4  This is soil. ☐

5  These are seeds. ☐

72

8 What is imagination?

Grammar: Present Simple: *want / need*, Affirmative and Negative

1. Read. Who doesn't need a pom-pom?

2. Read again and circle what the children need.

   pom-pom   glue   colored paper   yarn   pencils   chairs

Grammar: Present Simple: *want / need*, **Affirmative and Negative**

We can use the present simple to talk about the things we want and the things we need.

He **wants** ice cream.

She **doesn't need** new clothes.

Affirmative	Negative
I **want** an apple.	I **don't want** a banana.
You **need** glue.	You **don't need** crayons.
He **needs** an umbrella.	He **doesn't need** rain boots.
She **wants** a new kite.	She **doesn't want** a new bicycle.
We **need** aprons.	We **don't need** help.
They **want** some French fries.	They **don't want** water.

3 Read and match.

1 He doesn't want paint.
2 We don't want books.
3 I don't want an apple.
4 She doesn't want roller skates.
5 They don't want toys.
6 You don't want a painting.

a I want an orange.
b They want a pet.
c He wants crayons.
d We want games.
e You want a drawing.
f She wants a bike.

4 Read and check ✓ the correct sentence.

a 1 His hair is long. He needs a haircut. ✓
   2 His hair is long. He need a haircut. ☐

b 1 We wants glue for our puppets. ☐
   2 We want glue for our puppets. ☐

c 1 I can do it! I don't need help. ☐
   2 I can do it! I doesn't need help. ☐

5 Look and complete the sentences with *need*, *needs*, *don't need*, or *doesn't need*.

a They __need__ paper.
b They _____ a ruler.
c They _____ glue.
d They _____ paint.

e He _____ scissors.
f He _____ glue.
g He _____ crayons.

6 Write sentences about what you want or need. Use the words from the boxes.

~~wet~~   sad   ~~bored~~   thirsty   hungry   sunny

some sunglasses   a hug   some juice   some candy   ~~a towel~~   ~~a new game~~

a I'm __wet__. __I need a towel__.
b I'm __bored__. __I want a new game__.
c I'm _____. _____.
d I'm _____. _____.
e I'm _____. _____.
f It's _____. _____.

Grammar: Present Simple: *want / need*, Wh- Questions

YOUR SCHOOL NEEDS YOU!

Billy, when is the school's craft sale?
The craft sale is at the end of the school year.

Why do we need a craft sale?
The school needs some money. We can sell the crafts and make some money for the school.

What does the school need?
We need some new toys for recess. Things like balls, jump ropes, and hoops.

What can children make for the craft sale?
Children can make what they want. They can make animal masks, jewelry, ... anything!

What do the children need for their crafts?
They don't need anything. We have everything here: yarn, beads, glue, paint, cardboard. Children can come to the art room every afternoon and make something.

1 Read. Where can the children make their crafts?

2 Read and match.
1. When is the school craft sale?
2. What does the school need?
3. What crafts can the children make?
4. What do the children need for the crafts?
5. When can the children make the crafts?

a. Some new toys.
b. They don't need anything.
c. At the end of school year.
d. Every afternoon.
e. What they want.

Grammar: Present Simple: *want / need*, *Wh-* Questions

We can ask *Wh-* questions using *want* and *need*.

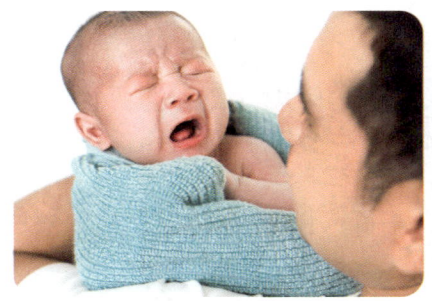  

What does the baby **want?**
He **wants** some milk.

What does Grandma **need?**
She **needs** some help.

What do the children **want?**
They **want** a drink.

3 Look and read. Then, write the answers.

> a drink   some paint   ~~some tape~~   some food

a. What does the boy need?
He needs some tape.

b.  What does the girl want?
_____

c.  What do the cats want?
_____

d.  What do the children need?
_____

4 Read and circle *do* or *does*.

a What **(does)** / **do** the teacher need?   She needs a piece of chalk.
b What **does** / **do** the plants need?   They need some water.
c What **does** / **do** the children need?   They need some glue.
d What **does** / **do** the school need?   It needs some new books.

77

5 **Complete the questions with *do* or *does*. Then, match the answers.**

1. What _____does_____ the girl need?   a A nap.
2. What _____ the boys need?   b A cloth.
3. What _____ the teacher want?   c Some tape.
4. What _____ they want?   d Aprons.

6 **Unscramble and write the questions and answers.**

a    b    c    d

a does / want? / she / What
What does she want? She wants a kite.

b  want? / What / he / does
_____

c  What / want? / do / they
_____

d  does / she / want? / What
_____

Learn to Write

Adjectives

We use adjectives to describe places, things, and people.

The school cafeteria is big.

These piñatas are colorful.

My grandma is smart and nice.

1 Look at the words. Circle the adjectives and underline the verbs.

> (imaginary)   grow   learn   angry   have   big
> colorful   read   thirsty   make   busy   scary

2 Complete the sentences with some of the adjectives above.

a The teacher is _____angry_____ when the students don't listen.

b Audrey likes to paint _____ pictures of flowers.

c The mall is _____ on weekends, when lots of people shop.

d The sculpture of the giraffe is very _____.

3 Underline the adjectives. Then, rewrite the sentences with an opposite adjective.

a My aunt is old.   _My aunt is young._

b This is an ugly mask.   _____

c It's really hot today!   _____

d The craft box is empty.   _____

Writing

1. Look at the pictures. Then, read the texts, and circle the adjectives.

a These are origami elephants. They are made of paper. They are (yellow) and orange. Real elephants are big, but these elephants are small.

b This is a painting of fruit. There are berries and cherries in a bowl. The cherries are red. Some of the berries are red, and some are black. They look delicious, but you can't eat them!

c These are flowers. They are made of colorful paper. They are very tall! The glitter makes these flowers beautiful!

d This is a horse made from balloons. They are red and blue. The horse has four legs, a long tail, and a big mane. It looks friendly.

2. Read again and complete the sentences with words from the box.

> delicious   balloons   ~~elephants~~   beautiful
> has   long   are   small

a These are origami (noun) ___elephants___.
   They are (adjective) _____.

b There (verb) _____ berries and cherries in a bowl.
   They look (adjective) _____.

c The glitter makes these flowers (adjective) _____.

d The horse is made from (noun) _____. It (verb) _____ four legs, a (adjective) _____ tail, and a big mane.

3) **Write some things you need to make the crafts in Activity 1.**

   a You need yellow and ____orange____ paper.

   b You need red and _____ paint.

   c You need _____ and glitter.

   d You need red and blue _____.

4) **Look at the pictures. Choose one and complete the sentences. Use the words or ideas in Activities 1 and 2.**

piñata

alebrije

This is a picture of a(n) (craft) _____. It is a (animal) _____.

It is colorful. It is (adjective) _____ and (adjective) _____.

It (verb) _____ four legs.

It looks (adjective) _____.

It is made of (noun) _____.

I think it is very (adjective) _____!

5) **What is your favorite craft?**

My favorite craft is _____.

You need _____ to make it.

I like it because it is _____.

CHECK

Did you ... • use nouns, verbs, and adjectives to describe a picture?

Practice Your Exam Skills

Look and read. Write *Yes* or *No*.

Examples

The desks are tidy.   No

The children are happy.   Yes

Questions

1 The children are all making crafts.

2 It's a very hot day.

3 The teacher is thirsty.

4 The girl in the orange T-shirt is painting a ladybug.

5 The blue bottles of paint are full.

9 Why do we need clothes?

Grammar: Present Progressive: Affirmative and Negative

Hi Grandma,

We're camping near a beach. The beach is very beautiful. We sleep in a big tent, and every day we eat outside. It's fun!

The sun is shining here, and it's very hot. I'm wearing my swimsuit and listening to the radio.

Dad and Alex are fishing right now. Mom isn't fishing—she's resting under a tree. She can't sleep well in the tent.

See you soon!

Mel xxx

1 **Read. What is Mel doing?**

2 **Read again and circle *True* or *False*.**

a	The family is camping near a beach.	(True) False
b	Mel is wearing a sweater now.	True False
c	Mel's mom is resting.	True False
d	Mel's dad and Alex are resting.	True False

83

Grammar: Present Progressive: Affirmative and Negative

We use the present progressive to talk about what is happening now.
We use *am*, *is*, and *are* with a verb + *-ing*.
  We're camping near the ocean.
We can make negative statements, too.
  She isn't reading her book.

Affirmative	Negative
I'm building a snowman.	I'm not making a sandcastle.
You're walking to school.	You aren't riding your bike.
She's playing with her friends.	He isn't playing with me.
We're helping to make dinner.	We aren't playing with our friends.
They're taking off their coats.	They aren't taking off their scarves.

Spelling Rules

put ⟶ putting
take ⟶ taking
ride ⟶ riding

3 Look and read. Check ✓ the correct answer

a

1 I'm collecting the leaves. ☐
2 We're collecting the leaves. ☐

b

1 She isn't jumping in puddles ☐
2 She's jumping in puddles. ☐

c

1 She's wearing sneakers. ☐
2 She's wearing boots. ☐

d

1 They're playing soccer. ☐
2 They aren't playing soccer. ☐

4 Look and complete with *is*, *isn't*, *are*, or *aren't*.

a They ____are____ playing with balloons.
b She _____ wearing a princess costume.
c He _____ waving goodbye!
d She _____ wearing shoes.
e He _____ drinking.
f They _____ dancing to the music.

5 Read, follow, and complete.

> We're wearing   She's wearing   He's wearing   ~~They're wearing~~

1 It's sunny.

2 It's rainy.

3 It's cold.

4 It's hot.

a _____ boots.

b _____ a T-shirt.

c _They're wearing_ sunglasses.

d _____ gloves.

Grammar: Present Progressive: *Yes/No* Questions

A Rainy Day

"Is it raining, Mom?" asks Tom.

"Yes, it is," Mom says.

"I don't want to play this game anymore. Let's play Hide-and-Seek," says Tom.

"OK! You count!" says Eddy.

Tom counts, and Eddy looks for somewhere to hide.

"Ready or not, here I come!" shouts Tom, and he goes upstairs to look.

Is Eddy hiding behind the door? No, he isn't.

Is Eddy hiding under the bed? No, he isn't.

"Found you!" shouts Tom suddenly. Eddy is hiding under the desk.

"Listen! Is Mom coming upstairs?" says Eddy.

"Yes, she is," says Tom. "Let's hide!"

"Tom, Eddy, it's lunchtime!" shouts Mom. "Where are you? Are you two hiding?"

"Yes, we are. Boo!" shout Tom and Eddy, as they both jump out from under the desk.

1 Read the story. Where is Eddy hiding?

2 Read and match.

1 Is it raining?
2 Is Tom counting?
3 Is Eddy hiding behind the door?
4 Are Eddy and Tom hiding from Mom?
5 Is their mom looking for the boys downstairs?

a Yes, he is.
b Yes, they are.
c No, she isn't.
d No, he isn't.
e Yes, it is.

Grammar: Present Progressive: *Yes/No* Questions

We make *Yes/No* questions about what is happening now.
We use *Is* and *Are* and a verb + *-ing*.

Are you **hiding**?
Yes, I **am**.

Is he **drawing**?
No, he **isn't**.

Questions	Affirmative Short Answers	Negative Short Answers
Are you wearing new jeans?	Yes, I am.	No, I'm not.
Is he playing Hide-and-Seek?	Yes, he is.	No, he isn't.
Is she taking off her coat?	Yes, she is.	No, she isn't.
Is it raining?	Yes, it is.	No, it isn't.
Are they putting on gloves?	Yes, they are.	No, they aren't.

3 Complete the questions. Then, circle the correct answer.

> snowing   ~~riding~~   wearing   making

a Is she ____riding____ a bike?

Yes, she is. / No, she isn't.

b Are they _____ party costumes?

Yes, they are. / No, they aren't.

c Is she _____ cookies?

Yes, she is. / No, she isn't.

d Is it _____ ?

Yes, it is. / No, it isn't.

4) **Look and complete the questions and answers with *is*, *isn't*, *are*, or *aren't*.**

a _____Is_____ the young boy wearing a hat? Yes, he _____is_____.
b _____ the parents at the table eating? No, they _____.
c _____ it raining? No, it _____.
d _____ the older children playing soccer? No, they _____.

5) **Look again at the picture in Activity 4 and write the short answers.**

a Is the little girl playing with a ball? _____Yes, she is._____
b Is the squirrel climbing the tree? _____
c Are the two boys jumping rope? _____
d Are the birds flying? _____

6) **Unscramble the questions. Then, write answers.**

a you / jeans? / Are / wearing
   Are you wearing jeans? Yes, I am.
b today? / Is / raining / it
   _____
c sitting / Are / you / friends? / with your
   _____
d your teacher / Is / now? / speaking
   _____

Learn to Write

Adverbs

An adverb describes how we do something. We use an adverb to say how an action happens.

We make most adverbs by adding *ly* to an adjective.

She is drawing carefully.

They are playing happily.

He is running quickly.

1 Read. Underline the **adverbs** in **red** and underline the **adjectives** in **green**.

a The <u>naughty</u> boy closes the door <u>angrily</u>.
b I'm wearing warm clothes.
c She's getting dressed slowly.
d These jeans are long.
e I'm hot. I need a drink.
f The children are playing happily in the garden.

Spelling Rules

careful ⟶ carefully
happy ⟶ happily
angry ⟶ angrily

2 Complete the sentences with adverbs. Make the adverbs from these adjectives.

quiet   loud   ~~slow~~   quick

a Max is tired. He's waking up _____slowly_____.
b Eda is singing _____.
c Don't talk. Please work _____ on the project.
d Slow down! You're talking very _____.

Writing

1 Read and underline the adverbs. Then, complete the table below.

This is a photo of me and my sister.
I'm wearing a pink coat.
We're on vacation in the mountains.
We're skiing carefully!
Look—the sky is so blue, and the sun is shining brightly.

	Mouna	Karl
A photo of:	me and my sister	me and my classmates
I'm wearing:		blue pants
We're (place):		in the country
We're (action + adverb):		drawing pictures quietly
Look:		a big field

2 Look at the table in Activity 1 to complete the text about Karl's photo.

a This is a photo of <u>me and my classmates</u>.
   I'm wearing _____
b We're on a school trip _____.
c We're _____.
d Look—you can see _____.

3) **Find a photo of yourself on vacation. Complete the table with notes.**

A photo of:	me
I'm wearing:	
We're (place):	
We're (action + adverb):	
Look:	

4) **Now use the information from Activity 3 to write about your photo.**

This is a photo of _____.

I'm wearing _____.

We're _____

_____.

We're _____

_____.

Look—you can see _____

_____.

CHECK

Did you … • use adverbs to describe actions? ☐

Practice Your Exam Skills

Look at the pictures and read the questions. Write one- or two-word answers.

Example

Where are the people?   In a ____store____.

Questions

1 How many people are there?   _____.

2 What is Mom wearing?   A blue _____.

3 Is the girl bored?   Yes, she _____.

4 What is Dad doing?   Giving a hat to _____.

5 Why is the boy crying?   He dropped his _____.

Review: Units 1–3

Read and choose words from the box to complete the text.

This is my best friend, Zac. He's from Canada, and he's ___seven___ years old. Zac has a big family. He has three **1** _____ and two sisters.

Zac lives **2** _____ the park in a big house. There are five bedrooms! There is also a big garden.

I see Zac at **3** _____ every day. Our school isn't big. There are 50 students and three **4** _____. There is a **5** _____. This is my favorite part of the school!

Example

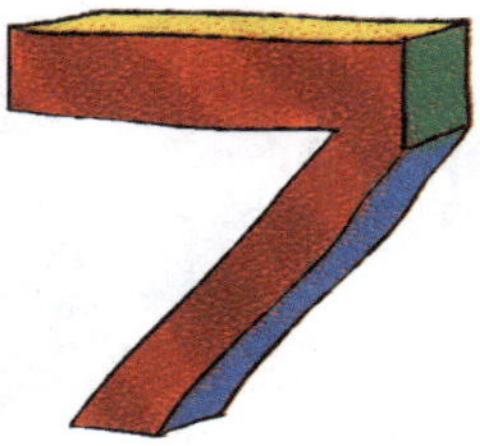

| seven | brothers | playground | school |

| teachers | next to | trees | under |

Review: Units 4–6

Read and choose words from the box to complete the text.

My weekend

On Saturday, I help my parents ____clean____ the house. I clean my room and pick up all of my **1** _____ . In the afternoon, we go for a picnic. We take food with us and **2** _____ sandwiches. Sometimes, we see trash on the ground. We pick it up and put it in the **3** _____.

On Sunday, I go to my friend Jonathan's house. We play with his toys. He doesn't have a **4** _____, so we go to the park sometimes. We like playing soccer and flying **5** _____ in the park.

Example

clean

balloons

toys

share

kitchen

trash can

kites

backyard

Review: Units 7–9

Read and choose words from the box to complete the text.

I am with my family at the zoo. There are giraffes, elephants, penguins, bats, and alligators.

The penguins are __swimming__. They can swim, but they can't fly. They need water and 1 _____ . There is some snow next to the water.

The giraffes are 2 _____ leaves from the trees. The giraffes are very 3 _____ . The alligator is walking to the pond. It wants to drink some water. A few bats are 4 _____ . You can see more bats at 5 _____ .

Example

swimming	tall	short	night

flying	snow	running	eating

95

Thanks and Acknowledgments

The authors and publishers acknowledge the following sources of copyright material and are grateful for the permissions granted. While every effort has been made, it has not always been possible to identify the sources of all the material used or to trace all copyright holders. If any omissions are brought to our notice, we will be happy to include the appropriate acknowledgments on reprinting and in the next update to the digital edition, as applicable.

Photography

All the photographs are sourced from Getty Images.

Cover photography by onurdongel/iStock/Getty Images; Mo Elnadi/Moment/Getty Images; zhihao/Moment/Getty Images; Javier Zayas Photography/Moment/Getty Images; Jess Yu/Moment/Getty Images; Yevhen Borysov/Moment/Getty Images; CHUYN/iStock/Getty Images.

Illustration

Collaborate Agency.

Cover illustrations by Ayesha Lopez (Advocate).

Typesetting

Blooberry Design and QBS Learning.